Nikon D3500 User Handbook

The Complete D3500 Manual with Illustrations for Beginners

By

Walt Leaburn

Copyright © 2023 Walt Leaburn,

All rights reserved

Nikon D3500 User Handbook

Table of Contents

Chapter 1: Getting the Lay of the Land 6
Getting Comfortable with Your Lens 6
    Attaching a lens.. 6
    Removing a lens 8
    Using a VR (vibration reduction) lens 9
    Setting the focus mode (auto or manual) 10
    Zooming in and out.. 12
Working with Memory Cards.. 12
Exploring External Camera Controls................................... 14
Restoring Default Settings 18

Chapter 2: Taking Great Pictures, Automatically . 19
Getting Good Point-and-Shoot Results 19
    Use proper lighting for professional photography...... 19
    Use filters and presets for professional photography. 19
Using Flash in Automatic Exposure Modes.......................... 20
Exploring Your Automatic Exposure Options 20
    Auto mode.. 20
    Scene modes... 20
Changing the (Shutter Button) Release Mode 22

Chapter 3: Controlling Picture Quality and Size...23
Considering Resolution (Image Size)..................................... 23
    Pixels and print quality... 23
    Pixels and screen display size 24
    Pixels and file size 24
Understanding the Image Quality Options............................ 25

JPEG: The imaging (and Web) standard 25
NEF (RAW): The purist's choice 27
Setting Image Size and Quality.................................30

Chapter 4: Reviewing Your Photos 31

Setting Playback Timing Preferences 31
   Adjusting playback timing 31
   Adjusting and disabling instant review 31
Enabling Automatic Picture Rotation 32
Viewing Images in Playback Mode............................33
   Viewing multiple images at a time 33
   Displaying photos in the Calendar view 35
   Zooming in for a closer view.. 36
Viewing Picture Data 39
   File Information mode.. 39
   RGB Histogram mode... 40
   Reading a Brightness histogram...................................41
   Understanding the RGB histograms 42
   Highlight display mode... 43
   Shooting Data display mode 43
   Overview Data mode.. 45
Deleting Photos 46
   Deleting images one at a time..................................... 46
   Deleting all photos 46
   Deleting a batch of selected photos 47
Protecting Photos 50

Chapter 5: Getting Creative with Exposure and Lighting 53

Introducing the Exposure Trio: Aperture, Shutter Speed, and ISO 53
   Understanding exposure-setting side effects 53
   Doing the exposure balancing act. 55
Exploring the Advanced Exposure Modes 56
Reading (And Adjusting) the Meter 56
Setting ISO, Aperture, and Shutter Speed 58
   Adjusting the aperture and shutter speed 58
   Controlling ISO 60
Choosing an Exposure Metering Mode 63
Applying Exposure Compensation 65

Chapter 6: Putting It All Together 67
Setting Up for Specific Scenes 67
   Shooting still portraits 67
   Capturing action 70
   Capturing scenic vistas 74
   Capturing dynamic close-ups 79

Chapter 7: Downloading, Organizing, and Archiving Your Picture Files 83
Sending Pictures to the Computer 83
   Connecting the camera and computer 83
   Starting the transfer process 84
Downloading and Organizing Photos with the Nikon Software 85
   Downloading with Nikon Transfer 85
   Viewing picture metadata 88
Processing RAW (NEF) Files 89
   Processing RAW images in the camera 89

Processing RAW files in ViewNX 92

Chapter 1: Getting the Lay of the Land

Getting Comfortable with Your Lens

Attaching a lens

Whatever lens you decide on, adhere to these instructions to secure it to the camera body:

1. Before removing the cap covering the lens mount on the front of the camera, turn it off.

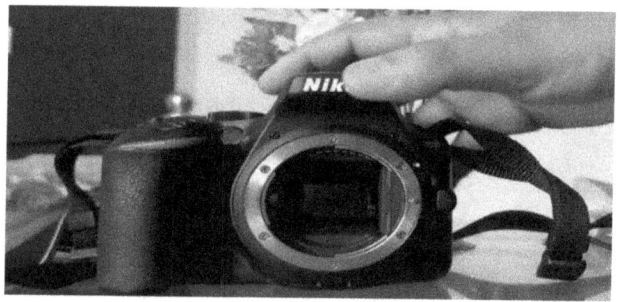

2. Take off the cap covering the lens's back.

3. Align the lens's tiny white dot with the corresponding dot on the camera body by holding the lens in front of the camera.

   The mounting index is the official name for those two little white dots.

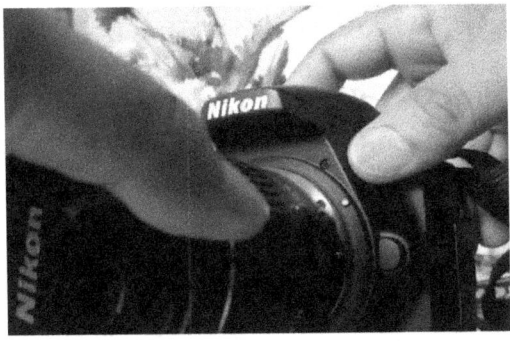

4. Place the lens on the camera's lens mount while maintaining the dots' alignment.

   Grip the lens by its back collar (the non-moving portion) rather than the movable forward end of the lens barrel when doing so.

5. Rotate the lens counterclockwise until it clicks into position.

   In other words, turn the lens toward the side of the camera that has the shutter button.

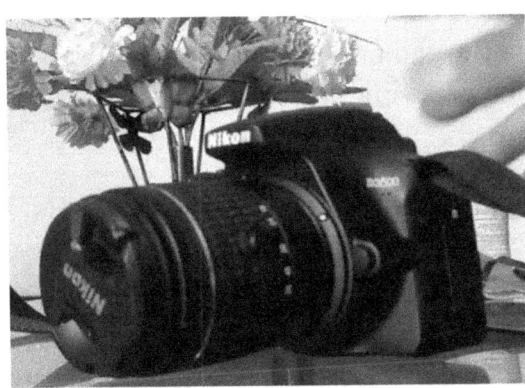

6. On a lens with an aperture ring, turn it to the highest f-stop number and lock it in place.

   If your lens has an aperture ring, xyz ache consults your lens manual to learn how to use it.

Removing a lens

Follow these steps to separate a lens from the camera body:

1. First, locate the lens-release button after turning off the camera.

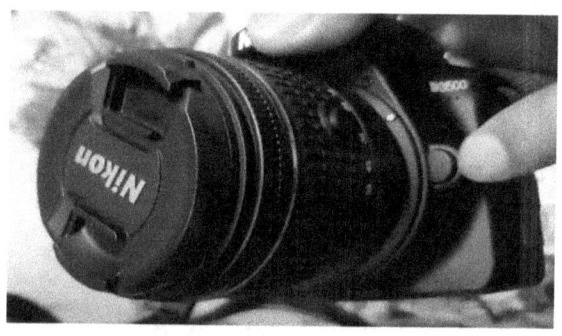

2. When the mounting index on the lens and the index on the camera body is lined up, press the lens-release button while rotating the lens clockwise (in the direction of the button).

   In other words, arrange the tiny white dots in a row.

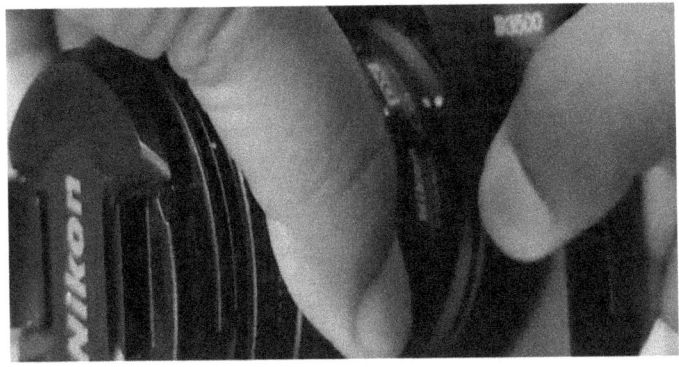

3. Attach the lens's back with the rear protective cap.

Cover the lens mount with the protective cap that comes with your camera, even if you aren't adding a new lens.

Using a VR (vibration reduction) lens

An image stabilization technique called vibration reduction (VR) reduces blur by camera shake. A VR NIKKOR lens can produce sharp photos up to four stops slower than a non-VR lens when utilizing a physically large NIKKOR lens or in low light or windy circumstances. Based on CIPA standards, this amount of f/stops will vary depending on the lens. The value is obtained by mounting an FX-format compatible lens on an FX-format D-SLR camera and setting the zoom lenses to their full telephoto position or by mounting a DX-format compatible lens on a DX-format D-SLR camera and setting the zoom lenses to their full telephoto position.

Since Nikon VR is a lens-based rather than an image sensor-based technology, algorithms are tailored to a particular lens. Another benefit of lens-based VR is that when you click the shutter release button halfway, a different algorithm validates the stabilization effect, giving you more freedom to create your photo. In addition, the system can recognize when a tripod is being used and panning is taking place (in which case you wouldn't want the lens to compensate for movement). Finally, it can address the specific shake brought on by the recurring vibration patterns created when taking pictures from a moving vehicle.

Nikon VR lenses feature two angular velocity sensors; one detects vertical motion (pitch), the other detects horizontal motion (yaw), and both sensors together handle diagonal motion. The sensors send information about angular velocity to a lens-mounted microcomputer, which calculates how much correction is required to counteract camera shake. Then, the microcomputer sends that information to a pair of voice coil motors, which move specific lens elements to make up for the detected motion.

Setting the focus mode (auto or manual)

Using an AF-P or an AF-S lens, the other lens that works with your camera, affects how you move between autofocusing and manual focusing. Here is the lowdown:

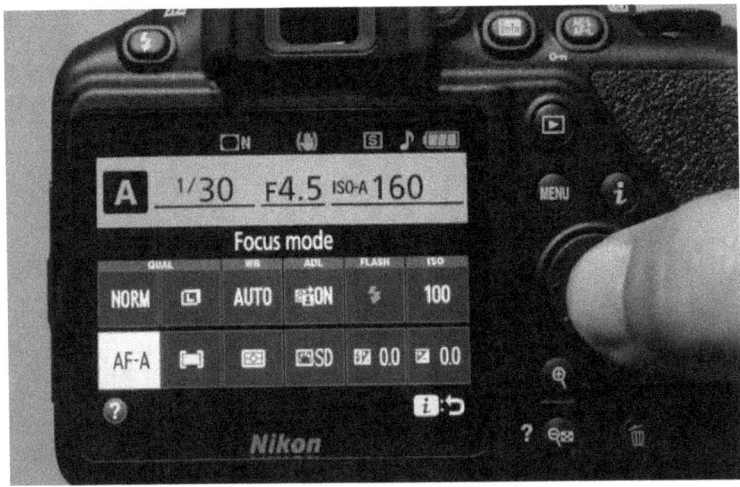

- **AF-P lens:** Change the focusing strategy using the Focus Mode setting on an AF-P lens. The control strip is the quickest way to reach the option, but you may also do it from the second page of the Shooting menu. In either case, choose MF (Manual Focus) to switch from automatic to manual focusing.

  Return to the Focus mode setting and select one of the AF (autofocus) options to resume autofocusing. Your exposure mode and whether you're working in Live View mode or framing your photographs with the viewfinder will determine how many AF settings are available.

- **AF-S lenses:** These lenses have an external switch that allows users to choose between automatic and manual focusing. The switch is turned to the A setting for automatic focusing and M for manual focusing. In addition, some lenses have a switch position marked

AF/M, allowing you to use autofocusing to set the initial focus and then fine-tune focus manually without moving the switch. Other lenses have switches marked AF and MF.

Zooming in and out

You can move a zoom ring if you purchase a zoom lens. Rotate the ring to zoom in or out on this lens. (Instead, some lenses have a push-pull mechanism that allows you to zoom by pushing and pulling the lens in either direction.)

Working with Memory Cards

The memory card is essential for your camera because it is the storage medium for your image files. Therefore, adhere to this advice for purchasing and caring for cards:

- **Buying SD cards:** Regular SD cards, which provide less than 4GB of storage space, SDHC cards (4GB-32GB), and SDXC cards are available for purchase (more than 32GB). The SD speed class specification should also be considered, as it describes how quickly data may be transferred to and from the card in addition to card capacity. There are numerous ways to determine card speed. The most used specification is called SD Speed Class, and it rates cards from 2 to 10, with 10 being the quickest. Most cards also have a second designation, such as UHS-1, -2, or 3. UHS (Ultra High Speed) is a new technology that increases data transmission speeds above the typical Speed Class 10 rate. You can tell the UHS rating by the number inside a small U symbol—UHS-3 is the fastest. However, remember that while UHS-2 and UHS-3 cards are compatible with the D3500, doing so has no performance benefits. The UHS-1 card speed is the maximum speed that the D3500 is capable of. Some SD cards are also evaluated based on how well they record video and precisely the number of frames per second they can record. A higher video-speed number denotes a quicker card, just like the conventional Speed Class and UHS ratings.

- **Formatting a card:** You must format a memory card before using it for the first time or insert one previously used in another device. It is because it will get the card ready to record your photos. Additionally, you must format the card if you notice the blinking letters FOR in the viewfinder or a message asking for formatting on the monitor.

- **Removing a card:** Switch the camera off after ensuring the memory card access light is off, signifying that the most recent photo you took has finished recording. Open the memory card door, apply a light downward pressure to the card, and then release. The card partially emerges from the slot, allowing you to remove it by grabbing the tail.

- **Handling cards:** Avoid touching the card's gold contacts on the back. When not in use, keep cards in their protective packaging or a memory card wallet. Avoid exposing cards to excessive cold or heat.

- **Locking cards:** You can lock your card by flipping the little switch, stopping any data from being recorded or wiped. A message appears on the LCD, and the Cd symbol blinks in the viewfinder if you insert a locked card into the camera.

- **Using Eye-Fi memory cards:** Your camera is compatible with Eye-Fi memory cards, which are specialized cards that let you wirelessly transfer files to devices like your computer.

Exploring External Camera Controls

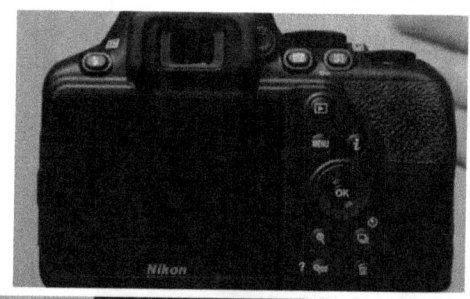

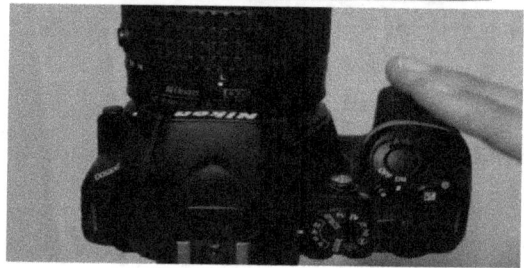

Mode dial: The exposure mode, which influences how much control you have over photo settings, is set via the mode dial. Opt for P, S, A, or M to have the most control.

On/Off switch/Shutter button: Turn the switch to turn the camera on; turn it again to turn it off. Press the shutter button. To activate autofocusing and activate the camera's exposure meter. To take a photo, press one more time.

Live View switch: Rotate the camera toward the back and release it to turn on and off Live View.

Command dial: Press a camera button to change several settings.

Exposure Compensation button: Press the Exposure Compensation button while turning the Command dial to adjust exposure for the next photo or video you take. A picture appears brighter when the value is higher.

Flash button: Press the flash button to activate the built-in flash when the exposure setting is P, S, A, or M. Press the button and turn the Command dial to change the flash mode for exposure modes that support it. To change flash power, turn the Command dial while maintaining pressure on the Exposure Compensation buttons.

Viewfinder adjustment dial: To adapt the viewfinder's focus to your eyesight, turn the viewfinder adjustment dial. Press the shutter button halfway, then let go to complete this action. Then, as you turn the dial, pay attention to the shooting information at the bottom of the viewfinder screen. The scene in front of the lens will remain in focus as you keep rotating until the data appears to you to be the clearest.

Info button: Press the information button to toggle the shooting information screen on and off while using the viewfinder. When Live View is activated, push to switch between the several data-display options.

AE-L/AF-L/Protect button: During shooting, click the AE-L/AF-L/Protect button to stop continuous exposure adjustment, locking in the current settings as long as you keep the button down. Continuous autofocusing also locks in the current focusing distance when used—Toggle file protection on and off while the recording is playing by pressing it.

Playback button: Press the playback button to turn on and off the video playback.

Menu button: Press the menu button to view the camera's menus. To access standard menus, turn the Mode dial to any mode other than Guide; menu panels will be guided in the Guide mode.

i button: The control strip, which provides quick access to essential shooting parameters, is accessed by pressing the I button while shooting. Press to bring up the i-button menu, which has a few post-capture options like retouching while an image is being played back.

Multi-selector/OK button: Press the outer edges up, down, left, and right to navigate menus and choose camera settings while shooting. Press OK to save your selections.

Press up or down to switch the playback display mode, then leave or right to scroll among the images.

Release-mode button: Pushing the Mode button To switch to shutter-release mode, press (single frame, continuous, or self-timer).

Zoom-in button: During Live View recording and image playback, use the Zoom-In button to enlarge the display. Press during movie playback to raise the audio volume.

Zoom Out/Thumbnails/Help: Press during Live View shooting to decrease on-screen magnification. To switch between full-frame playback, thumbnail view, and calendar view while in playback mode, push. Press the button when a question mark appears on a menu or information screen to show more details about the current operation.

Delete button: Press to delete the photos presently being shown or selected while looking through photos.

Lens-release button: Press the lens-release button to release the lens from the camera's lens mount and remove it.

Speaker/microphone: The camera records sound and plays it back through the speaker when you record audio for movies.

Connection port cover: Open this door to reveal the USB and HDMI ports.

Restoring Default Settings

Your Nikon D3500 camera needs to be reset to factory settings for several reasons, including when you want to sell it or when a system fault occurs. This explains how to return all setup menu settings, including the shooting settings, to their default positions.

1. Turn on your camera.

    Check the power of your camera.

2. To access the main menu, click the MENU button.

    The button is in the upper-left corner.

3. Select SETUP from the menu.

    Choose the i menu

4. Scroll down to the RESET ALL SETTINGS option on the SETUP menu.

    To access the menu, select OK.

5. Select YES to complete the factory reset when a confirmation message appears on the screen. Done!

Chapter 2: Taking Great Pictures, Automatically

Getting Good Point-and-Shoot Results

Use proper lighting for professional photography.

Let's start with lighting for product photography. With good lighting, your product will look as it does to you in person, and your background will be unique. " According to Tony Northrup in an article for the digital photography school, a white background without light doesn't seem white in the picture; it appears grey.

Lighting for product photography comes in two flavors: artificial and natural lighting. Which configuration you choose will depend on the product you're promoting. For example, products with edible products, people, and apparel can get photographed using natural lighting, and these shots with a natural appearance can get used in social media settings.

Use filters and presets for professional photography.

When you use filters in your photos, the photo looks too good, so the right filter and preset are also important. Every photographer should have the correct knowledge of the filters because the right filter plays a vital role in photos. The filter is good, but when you use too many filters, you will look terrible, so the conclusion is to use filters properly and correctly. Filter help minimize glare and reflections, reduce the light coming into the lens, and more. In addition, each lens filter serves a specific effect that can help enhance the final look of an image.

Using Flash in Automatic Exposure Modes

1. Select flash mode.

   Rotate the command dial while pressing the button until the chosen flash mode appears.

2. Take pictures.

Exploring Your Automatic Exposure Options

Auto mode

The camera examines the surroundings in both modes to determine the best settings for capturing the image. The only distinction between the two modes is the flash-disabling function of Auto Flash Off. In addition, several Flash modes are available in Auto mode.

Scene modes

When the Mode dial is set to Scene, automated exposure options for capturing particular subjects in ways regarded as ideal by photography tradition are available. For instance, skin tones are altered in Portrait mode to appear warmer and softer, and the background is blurred to highlight your subject. Likewise, greens and blues are more vivid in landscape mode, and the camera tries to keep nearby and faraway things crisp.

The upper-left corner of the screen displays an icon for the current Scene type. (If you are using Live View mode, you might need to hit the Info button to cycle between the different Live View displays until you find one that shows the icon.)

Rotate the Command dial to reveal a selection screen to access additional Scene modes. To move through the available scenarios, turn the dial or tap the arrows highlighted in the picture. Exit the selection screen by pressing the shutter button halfway and letting go when you find a scenario you want to try. Then, simply compose, focus, and fire after that.

The names of the Scene modes should give you enough information to figure out what they do, but if you're having trouble as you scroll through your choices, you may use the Zoom Out button to see a brief description of the mode's now chosen. Unfortunately, this technique only works while shooting through a viewfinder and not when using Live View.

The procedure for taking photos in the Scene modes is largely the same as for shooting in Auto mode. However, some Scene modes have various default configurations for Release mode, flash, and autofocusing.

Each time you push the shutter button, the camera either records a single image or a burst of photos as long as you hold down the shutter button or employs Self-Timer mode, which delays the image capture until a few seconds after you click the shutter button. The camera also has a Quiet Shutter option that muffles the standard shutter-release noises.

Changing the (Shutter Button) Release Mode

The Release mode setting allows you to choose whether you want to record a burst of photos as long as you hold down the shutter button (Continuous mode), record a single image each time you press the shutter button (Single Frame mode) or postpone the image capture for a few seconds after you press the shutter button. Additionally, a Quiet Shutter option muffles some shutter release noises.

The Information screen and Live View display icons to show what release mode is currently active. If your screen displays a different data collection, press the Info button to cycle through the available modes.

Pressing the Release Mode button will bring up the selection screen, where you can change the release mode setting. In Live View mode, the screen appears overlaid over the live display.

Chapter 3: Controlling Picture Quality and Size

Considering Resolution (Image Size)

Pixels and print quality

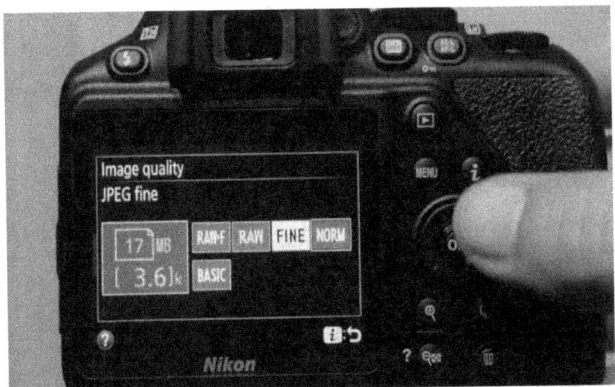

Since that is what the setting governs, I would rename the Image Quality option to File Type if I had my way. So let's get to it: The file type, often called a file format or a file extension, specifies how your image data is saved and recorded. Your decision impacts picture quality, but so do the Image Size setting and ISO settings. Beyond visual quality, your choice of file type also has implications. In any case, your camera offers two file types: JPEG and Camera Raw, or simply Raw. NEF (Nikon Electronic Format) is the name for this file type on Nikon cameras.

The benefits and drawbacks of each format are discussed in the next two sections. If you've already decided what you want, you may find out how to choose in the section under "Setting Image Size and Image Quality."

Pixels and screen display size

The quality of photographs seen on a monitor, television, or other screen device is not impacted by resolution the way it is for printed photos—instead, the size at which the image is determined by resolution. One of the most misunderstood aspects of digital photography is this one. For now, simply be aware that touchscreen photographs require significantly fewer pixels than printed ones. Unfortunately, in many email systems, even a Small resolution level produces images that are too large to be seen in full.

Pixels and file size

The quantity of information needed to make an image file grows with each additional pixel. Thus, an image with a higher resolution has a bigger file size than an image with a lower resolution.

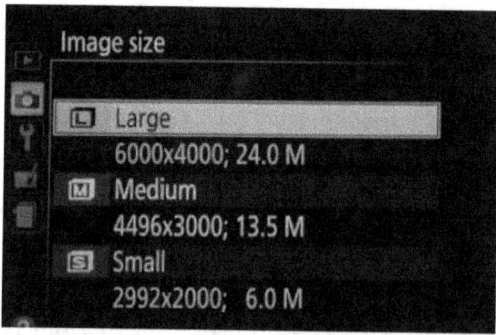

There are various issues with large files:

- You use up camera memory cards more quickly. Additionally, downloading photographs take up more room in the digital storage space you create, whether on a computer's hard drive or an online storage service (cloud storage).

- The camera needs more time to process and save the image data on the memory card after you hit the shutter button, so if you want to burn copies of your images on DVD, you need to buy a lot of blank DVDs. In addition, fast-action shooting may be hampered by this added delay.

- Larger images take longer to upload and download when you share photos online.

- Your computer requires more resources and processing time to process huge files when you edit photographs in your photo editing software.

Understanding the Image Quality Options

JPEG: The imaging (and Web) standard

This format, pronounced "jay-peg," is the default setting on your D3500 and most other digital cameras. JPEG's popularity stems from two key factors:

- **Immediate usability:** JPEG files may be viewed by all web browsers and email clients, allowing you to post photos online as soon as you take them. You can also print a JPEG file at any retail photo store. However, Raw (NEF) files must be converted into

JPEG or another standard format, such as TIFF, to be printed commercially.

JPEG files are less than Raw files in terms of file size. Additionally, smaller files take up less space on your computer's hard drive and your camera's memory card.

The drawback of JPEG is that it uses lossy compression to produce smaller files—you knew there had to be a drawback somewhere. Some image data is lost during this process. JPEG artifacting is a problem caused by excessive compression.

Fortunately, you can tell your camera how much compression you will tolerate. Three JPEG settings are available, and they yield the following outcomes:

- **JPEG Fine:** The file is four times smaller than it would otherwise be due to the compression ratio of 1:1. There shouldn't be many, if any, compression artifacts because minimal compression is used.

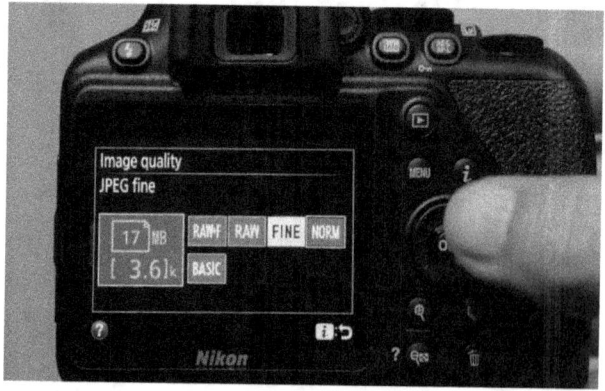

- **JPEG Normal:** 1:8 is the new compression ratio. There is also a higher possibility of encountering some artifacting. The default configuration is this one.

- **JPEG Basic:** It increases to a 1:16 compression ratio. That's a significant amount of compression, increasing the chance of artifacting.

But rot, even the Basic option, produces the level of artifacting you see. For you to notice artifacting and comprehend how it differs from the quality loss that happens when you have insufficient pixels, I emphasized the flaw in that case. In reality, you won't likely notice little of a quality difference between the Fine, Normal, and Basic compression levels if you keep the image print or display size small. Only when a shot is blown up significantly can the disparities stand out.

NEF (RAW): The purist's choice

Camera Raw, or simply Raw (as in uncooked), is the alternative image file type you can produce.

For three reasons, advanced, highly picky photographers favor raw:

- More creative freedom When you use JPEG, your camera's internal software adjusts your photographs' color, exposure, and sharpness as necessary to generate the outcomes Nikon thinks its consumers would like. The camera captures the raw, original image data when shooting in raw. The photographer makes selections regarding color, exposure, and other factors after copying the image file to the computer and using specialized software called a raw converter to create the final image. The D3500 and Nikon Capture NX-D, a free program that can be downloaded from the Nikon support website, include built-in Raw converters.

- **Higher bit depth:** The number of distinct color values that can get contained in an image file depends on the bit depth. The red, blue, and green color channels, which together make up a digital image, are limited to 8 bits each in JPEG files, for a total of 24 bits. That equals around 16.7 million color combinations. The D3500 uses 12 bits per channel to capture raw photos.

The 8-bit palette of 16.7 million values is more than enough, producing beautiful visuals, even though switching to 12 bits seems like a significant improvement. The extra bits may be helpful if you use your photo-editing tool to change the exposure, contrast, or color. The extra bits can occasionally prevent an issue known as banding or posterization, which causes sudden color breaks where smooth, seamless transitions should be visible when you make excessive modifications. (However, this issue is only sometimes avoided by using a greater bit of depth.)

- **Best image quality:** You avoid the risk of artifacting that might happen with JPEG because

Raw doesn't use the destructive compression associated with JPEG.

However, there are several drawbacks to using Raw:

- You can only do something with your photos once you process them using a Raw converter. They need to be included in text documents, multimedia presentations, or internet sharing. If you use Nikon Capture NX-D or Nikon ViewNX-i, two additional free photo applications from Nikon, you can view and print them immediately. You can also find apps for viewing Raw images on your smartphone or tablet. However, most apps and computer-based photo tools demand that you convert Raw data to a common format, like JPEG or TIFF. Raw files are often inaccessible to retail printing facilities as well.

- Compared to JPEGs, raw files are larger. It is because raw doesn't use lossy compression to compress files like JPEG. Additionally, the highest resolution is always used to capture raw files. For these reasons, raw files are much larger than JPEGs, taking up more space on your memory card and the hard drive or another picture-storage device.

Consider your photography demands, if you have the time and motivation to convert Raw files, and whether the benefits of Raw exceed the drawbacks.

Setting Image Size and Quality

You can choose from the following options to change the settings:

- **i button:** The screen where you may choose the desired setting will appear after pressing the I button, which you can use to access the display control strip, highlight one of the two selections, and then hit OK.

- **Shooting menu:** The Image Quality and Size settings can also be changed through the Shooting menu. The option for image size is underlined, and the one for image quality is located immediately upstairs.

The choices screen appears when you choose the Image Size option from the menu. The total number of pixels, expressed in megapixels, is represented by the second value for each setting. For example, 6000 x 4000 pixels translates to 24 megapixels, which is what is indicated as 24M on the Image Size options screen. Recall that 1 million pixels equal 1 megapixel. Check the displays you see when you choose Image Size and Image Quality through the control strip to see the file size in megabytes. The larger the file size and the fewer photographs you can place on your memory card, the higher the megapixel count.

Chapter 4: Reviewing Your Photos

Setting Playback Timing Preferences

Adjusting playback timing

The default setting for the monitor when the camera is in playback mode is for it to go off automatically five minutes after no activity. You can change the shutoff timing by accessing the Setup menu and choosing Auto Off Timers, which displays the screen. For the time being, disregard the first three options, which regulate the shutoff timing for several camera functions in addition to the playback shutoff. Choose Custom instead. Next, you can select playback shutoff times that range from 8 to 10 minutes.

Remember that the monitor uses much battery power, so keep the display time as brief as possible. Just keep in mind that, as the setting name suggests, this choice also regulates how long camera menus are shown before being automatically shut down.

Adjusting and disabling instant review

You can quickly review a shot using this option, which can be found in the Playback menu and is enabled by default, without switching from shooting mode to playback mode. Instead, the photo is displayed on the monitor for 4 seconds after the camera has finished recording it to the memory card.

The monitor displays some shooting information during the Image Review display, such as the exposure mode, the number of shots still to be taken, the battery status sign, and the Image Size and Quality of the photograph. In addition, the number of files on the memory card and the number of the frame you just snapped are displayed in the screen's upper-right corner; for instance, 4/15 indicates that you are currently seeing the fourth of 15 files on the card.

Enabling Automatic Picture Rotation

The camera retains the image orientation when you take a picture, regardless of whether you hold the camera. It usually takes a horizontally oriented image or turns it on its side to create a vertically oriented picture. Vertical images are rotated during playback, appearing upright after the camera reads the orientation data. When you examine the image in any photo-editing software that can read the data, the picture is automatically turned.

You can turn off rotation; in this case, vertically oriented images will look sideways. Next, open the Playback menu and select one of the two options listed below to regulate this playback function:

- **Auto Image Rotation:** This setting allows you to choose whether orientation information is stored in the image file. Choose Off to remove the data. Then, neither your photo program nor the on-camera playback of the image rotates the image.

- **Rotate Tall:** Using this setting, you can decide whether the camera considers the orientation information while playback is in progress. If you don't want the camera to rotate images with orientation data attached, select Off. (Even if Rotate Tall is set to On, images that are not labeled with the data do not rotate.)

Whatever settings you select, there is no rotation during the instant-review picture display. Neither are films rotated. Additionally, remember that shooting with the lens pointed straight up or down can occasionally confuse the camera and cause it to capture incorrect orientation data.

Viewing Images in Playback Mode

Viewing multiple images at a time

Instead of presenting each image or video one at a time, you can display 4, 9, or even 72 thumbnails.

This display option operates as follows:

- The Zoom Out button must be pressed to see thumbnails.

    Press once to switch between the single image view and the four thumbnail views, twice to the nine picture view, and once more to display the tiny thumbnails included in the 72 image view. The Calendar view, a useful function described in the following section, is accessible with one more press.

Fewer thumbnails will be shown if you click the Zoom In button.

When you click the Zoom In button, you may see each thumbnail at a bigger size while also returning from Calendar view to the usual thumbnail display or, if you're already there. Once more, pressing once reduces the number of thumbnails from 72 to 9, pressing twice reduces the number to 4, and pressing once more sends you back to the single image view.

- To choose an image or movie, move the yellow frame over it. You must first select an image before doing playback tasks, including removing a photo. The chosen image is enclosed in a yellow frame. Next, move the yellow frame over a different image using the Multi Selector or Command dial.

- Press the OK button to easily switch between the Full-Frame view and thumbnail display (globally change). Instead of wasting time continually hitting the Zoom In button to go back to the full-frame view, simply press OK. The chosen frame fills the entire screen. Unless the presently shown file is a movie, pressing OK initiates movie playback, and pressing OK again returns to the thumbnail display. Finally, press the Zoom Out button to return to the thumbnail view.

Scroll across the display by using the Multi Selector. Then, press up or down to the following or previous thumbnails screen.

The name of the folder containing the photos and the final four digits of the image or video filename is shown in the four- and nine-thumbnail displays. The filename and folder name appears at the screen's bottom in a 72-thumbnail view.

Displaying photos in the Calendar view

Using the calendar display mode, finding photos by the day you took them is simple.

1. Press the Zoom Out button to switch between the single-image, thumbnail, and calendar views as needed. Press the button four times to switch to Calendar view, for instance, if you are currently viewing photographs in full-frame view.

2. Drag the yellow highlight box over a date with an image using the Multi Selector or Command dial.

   (The month's number can be seen above the year to the right of the top of the screen.) The first few photos taken on the given date are shown as thumbnails on the right side of the screen. However, until you complete the subsequent step, you cannot scroll the thumbnail display to see all the photos taken on the day or choose a single photo.

3. Press the Zoom Out button to bring up the thumbnail strip, allowing you to view and choose any photo shot on the selected date.

By pressing the Multi Selector up and down or turning the Command dial, you can scroll between the thumbnails in the vertical thumbnail strip after you hit the button. As you scroll the display, the yellow frame shifts from one thumbnail to the next, indicating which one is the presently selected file.

4. Press and hold the Zoom In button to momentarily enlarge the selected image.

   The huge preview vanishes when you release the button, and the calendar reappears. You can scroll to and enlarge another image if necessary because the thumbnail strip is still the display section currently in use.

5. Press the Zoom Out button to return to the calendar side of the display and choose a different date.

   You can repeatedly click the button to switch between the thumbnail strip and the calendar side of the display as often as you like.

6. Select the desired image in the thumbnail strip to switch from Calendar view to single-image view. Then click OK.

Zooming in for a closer view

After displaying a photo in a single-frame view, you can magnify it. In addition, you can zoom in on still images; however, this feature isn't available for movies.

To shift from thumbnail view to single-image view, select the photo and then press OK. If the display is in Calendar view, press OK twice.

After the photo is onscreen all by its lonesome, try these magnification features:

- **Magnify the image.** Press the Zoom In button. You can magnify the image to a maximum of 19 to 38 times its original display size, depending on the resolution (pixel count). Just keep pressing the button until you reach the magnification you want. (Notice the plus-sign magnifying glass symbol on the button, indicating zoom-in.)

- **Reduce magnification.** Press the Zoom Out button, which sports the minus sign magnifying glass. (That gridlike thing next to the magnifying glass reminds you that the button also comes into play when you want to go from a full-frame view to a thumbnail view.

- **View another part of the magnified picture.** When an image is magnified, a thumbnail showing the entire image appears in the lower-right corner of the screen. The yellow frame in this picture-in-picture image indicates the area currently consuming the rest of the monitor space. (The white bar below the box indicates the zoom level; the bar turns green when you reach maximum magnification.) Use the Multi Selector to scroll the yellow box and display a different portion of the image. After a few seconds, the navigation thumbnail disappears; press the Multi Selector in any direction to redisplay it.

- **Inspect faces.** When you magnify portraits, the picture-in-picture thumbnail displays a white border around each face. If you press the i button, a mini-menu appears, offering two options, Face Zoom and Trim. Select Face Zoom, and you can then press the Multi Selector right or left to jump from face to face for a closer look. Finally, press the i button again to exit Face Zoom mode.

  When it works correctly, this is an excellent tool for checking for closed eyes, red eyes, and spinach in the teeth. Unfortunately, the camera sometimes fails to detect faces, especially if the subject isn't looking directly at the camera. And when the photo contains only a few faces, you may find it easier to simply move the magnification box around the screen without bothering with Face Zoom.

- **View more images at the same magnification.** While the display is zoomed, rotate the Command dial to display the same area of the next photo at the same magnification.

Crop the picture to the magnified view. When a picture is magnified, you can quickly create a second image that contains just the area currently visible on the monitor. In other words, you can do instant in-camera cropping. Your original is left intact; the camera makes a copy of the photo and crops the copy.

To perform this trick, press the i button to display the mini-menu above, but this time choose Trim. On the next screen, select Done to create the cropped copy. Check out the Trim function on the Retouch menu for other cropping options.

- Return to a full-frame view. You don't need to press the Zoom Out button until the entire photo is displayed. Instead, just press OK.

Viewing Picture Data

File Information mode

The monitor shows the information when in File Information mode. The key to understanding what data is displayed, from the top of the screen to the bottom:

•Frame Number/Number Frames: The first value in this field shows the frame number of the image now being viewed, while the second shows the total number of frames stored on the memory card. The frame count includes movies, with each clip counted as a single frame.

•Folder: Unless you make custom folders, a sophisticated trick you can investigate, folders are named automatically by the camera. The first folder produced by the camera has the designation 100D3500. When you go over that number, the camera creates a new folder and assigns the next folder number. Each folder can hold up to 9,999 images.

•Filename: The camera also gives your file names by default. Filenames conclude with a three-letter code that designates the file type, which for still photographs is either JPG (for JPEG) or NEF (for Raw). In addition, the camera employs the extension MOV for movie recordings and NDF for dust-off reference picture files, a sophisticated function explicitly made for Nikon Capture NX-D.

Filenames' initial four characters can also differ in the ways listed below:

•DSC_: You took the picture using the sRGB color space, which is the standard. This setting is the ideal option for most people for reasons you can explore.

• DSC: The underscore character appears first if you switch the Color Space setting to Adobe RGB. (By the way, you can't capture movies in this color space.)

RGB Histogram mode

Press the Multi Selector down to switch from Highlights mode to RGB Histogram mode, which shows your image. (Remember: You can only use this mode if you make it available via the Playback menu's Playback Display Options choice.)

The information below the thumbnail displays the shot's White Balance settings. The two number values indicate whether you fine-tuned that setting along the amber-to-blue (first value) or green-to-magenta (second value) axes. The first value indicates the setting (second value). Zeros indicate no finetuning. If you utilize the protected, retouched, rated, or send-to-smart-vice options on the picture you're looking at, you also see symbols for those tags.

You also get four histograms, which are charts. As indicated in the illustration, there are actually two different sorts of histograms: the RGB histogram, which consists of the top three, and the brightness histogram (RGB for red, green, and blue).

Reading a Brightness histogram.

By glancing at your image on the monitor and the blinkies in Highlights mode, you can get a general understanding of image exposure. Still, the Brightness histogram offers a more precise method.

The maximum tonal range in photography is represented by the horizontal axis of the histogram, which spans from the darkest shadows on the left to the brightest highlights on the right. Additionally, the vertical axis displays the number of pixels that fall at each brightness level. A spike shows an increase of pixels at that brightness value.

Remember that there is no "ideal" histogram you should strive for. Instead, consider how your subject's shadows, highlights, and mid-tones are distributed while interpreting the histogram. For instance, you would anticipate seeing a few shadows in a picture of a polar bear traversing a snowy terrain. However, pay close attention if you notice a dense concentration of pixels at the extremes of the histogram to the right or left, which can signify a badly overexposed or underexposed image, respectively.

Understanding the RGB histograms

In the RGB Histogram display mode, the Brightness histogram and the RGB histogram are visible.

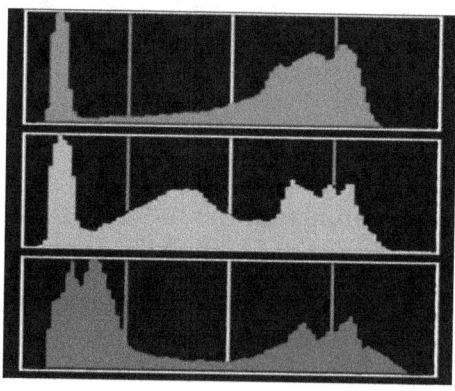

However, you learn more about color saturation than image brightness when looking at the brightness data for a single channel. (Saturation measures a color's purity; a saturated hue contains neither black nor white.) When red, green, and blue light are combined, and each component is at its brightest, white is the result. Black is produced when all three channels have no brightness. However, if you have as much red as possible without any blue or green, you have saturated red. Two channels combined at their highest brightness result in full saturation. Maximum red and blue, for instance, result in totally saturated magenta. Additionally, where colors are fully saturated, visual detail can be lost. For example, a rose petal that should be a flat glob of pure red has various shades from medium to dark red.

You can lose picture detail due to highly saturated colors if all the pixels for one or two channels are compressed to the right end of the histogram. But, because the highest red, green, and blue concentrations combine to form white, blown highlights may have occurred if all three channels have a dense pixel population at the right end of the histogram. Either way, you might want to change the exposure options and give it another shot.

A skilled RGB histogram reader can also identify problems with color balance by examining the pixel values. The view on the camera monitor makes it quite simple to spot issues with color balance, though.

Highlight display mode

In a photo-editing program, blown highlights, also known as clipped highlights in some quarters, are one of the trickiest issues to fix. Both words simply refer to highlights, the brightest parts of the image being overexposed to the point where sections that should have a range of light colors are completely white. For instance, overexposure causes pixels in a cloud image that should be light to very light gray to turn white, which reduces the amount of information in the clouds.

Shooting Data display mode

By pressing the Multi Selector up and down, you can scroll across numerous information screens while in Shooting Data mode.

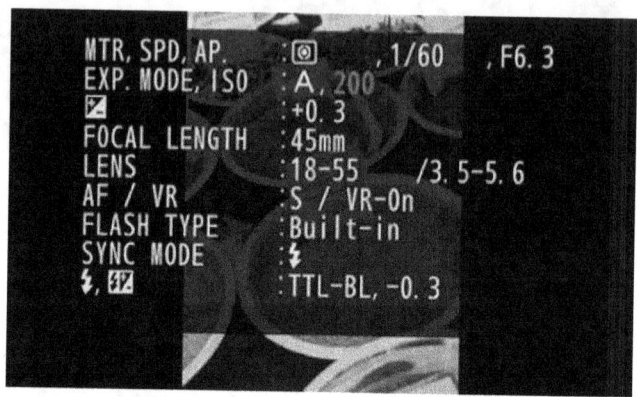

If you used the Protected and Send to Smart Device capabilities, those icons can be seen in the monitor's upper-left corner. And you can see the Retouch icon when you view an image that you edited using one of the camera's Retouch functions. The rating you gave appears in the lower-left corner of the screen if you activate the Rating option.

- The lower-right corner of the display shows the filename's current folder number and the last four characters.

- The camera overrode the ISO Sensitivity level you chose to create a decent exposure if the ISO value on Shooting Data Page 1 displays in red. This move happens only when automatic ISO adjustment is enabled in the P, S, A, and M exposure modes.

- If you use the Image Comment option on the Setup menu, the Comment item, which is the last item on the third Shooting Data screen, contains a value.

- The fourth screen shows if you add copyright information to your image.

- You can add location information to photos using the Nikon SnapBridge software and a compatible smartphone or tablet. Your smart gadget provides the data. The details appear on a different Shooting Data display screen if you choose this option. Although Nikon technically refers to this screen mode as Location Data mode, it is a part of the Shooting Data display mode. When the Shooting Data Mode is turned on, it is immediately enabled.

Overview Data mode

The playback screen in Overview mode includes a tiny image thumbnail, a ton of shooting data, and a Brightness histogram, though not nearly as much as in Shooting Data mode. You can enable and disable this display mode through the Playback Display Options setting on the Playback menu.

You may read more about how to interpret a brightness histogram in the prior section, "Reading a Brightness Histogram." You can find the Frame Number/Total Frames information in the picture thumbnail's upper-right corner (29/64 in the illustration). See the prior section, "File Information mode," for more information on that data. The symbols for the protect, retouch, rating, and send-to-smart-device capabilities only appear when they are appropriate for the photo or movie file you are viewing, just like with the other display modes.

Deleting Photos

Deleting images one at a time

The Delete button can remove movie and photo files while being played back. However, the procedure differs according to the active playback mode:

- Press the Delete button while in single-image view.

- In the thumbnail view, drag the yellow selection frame over the image you want to delete using the Multi Selector or Command dial. Next, click Delete.

- Mark the date that contains the file in Calendar view. After selecting the file's thumbnail with the Multi Selector using the Zoom Out button to access the thumbnail list, simply press Delete.

Afterward, a notice appears asking if you want to delete the picture. If you do, hit Delete once more. Then, simply click the Playback button to stop the procedure.

Deleting all photos

Open the Playback menu, choose Delete, and then hit OK. Then select All, and then click OK. Finally, select Yes and press OK when the camera asks you if you want to delete all of your photos and videos.

Deleting a batch of selected photos

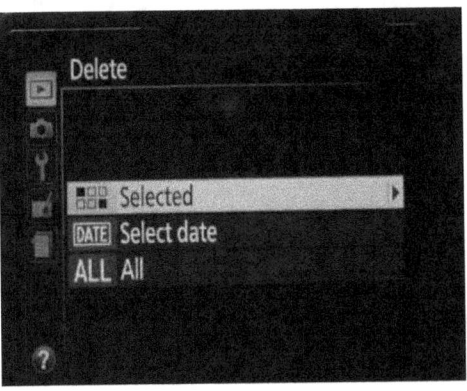

Avoid wasting time by wiping each file one at a time when you wish to delete more than a few files but not all of the images and videos on the card. Instead, you can mark multiple files for erasure and then move them all simultaneously to the trash.

Start by bringing up the Playback menu, select Delete, and then click OK. Next, you will see the screen that shows the panel that gives you two choices for choosing which files to delete:

- **Selected**

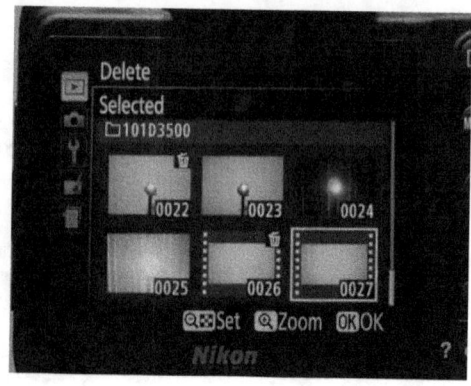

If the files you want to delete were all captured on different days, use this option. To view thumbnails, highlight Selected and push the Multi Selector's right button.

Place the yellow selection frame over the first file you want to delete using the Multi Selector, then click the Zoom Out button. The thumbnail's upper-right corner features a garbage bin. If you change your mind, use the Zoom Out button to remove the Delete tag. Then, press the Playback button to reverse the deletion of all your chosen files.

Hold down the Zoom In button to closely examine the chosen image. The display switches back to the standard thumbnail view when you let go of the button.

- **Select Date**

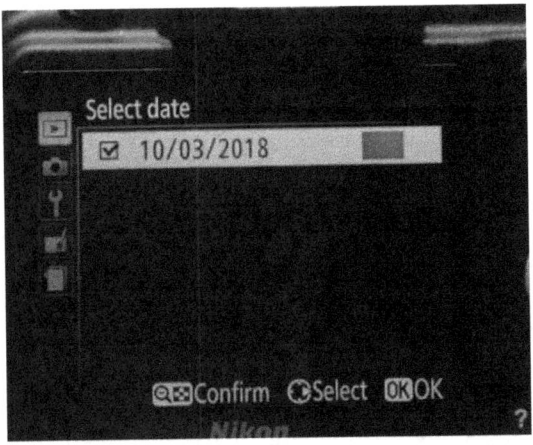

This option quickly erases any entry on a day you'd rather forget. Once you've selected Select Date, use the Multi Selector's right button to bring up a list of available dates. Next, press the Multi Selector to the right after selecting a date. All photos shot on that day are marked for deletion by a checkmark in the box next to the date. Press the Multi Selector to the right once more to remove the checkmark.

Need help remembering which pictures correspond to the date you chose? Use these strategies:

Press the Zoom Out button to see the thumbnails of every photo shot on the selected date. (Again, note the icon next to the word Confirm at the bottom of the screen; it resembles the icon on the Zoom Out button.)

Press the Zoom In button to see the selected thumbnail in full view momentarily. To return to the thumbnails screen, let go of the button.

- Press OK to choose the desired date for deletion and go back to the primary date list on the confirmation (thumbnails) page. Alternatively, you can press the Zoom Out button to return to the date list without picking a date.

Press OK after designating a deletion date or marking files for deletion. A confirmation message appears; choose Yes and click OK.

Protecting Photos

Giving files protected status will prevent unintentional erasure. The camera prevents you from deleting the file after this point, regardless of whether you push the Delete button or select the Delete option from the Playback menu.

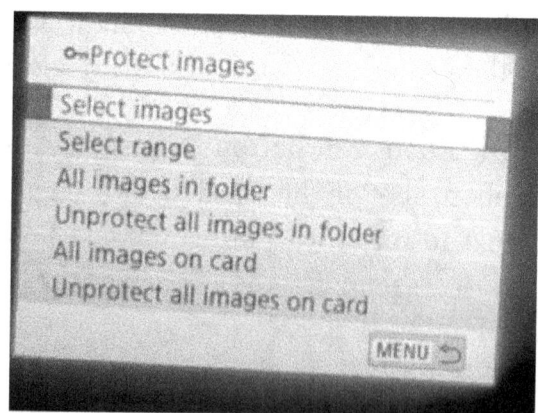

Keep in mind that locking a file prohibits you from rating it, so rate photos before giving them protected status. Also, the file cannot be edited using any of the tools in the Retouch menu.

Take these actions to safeguard a file:

1. First, make the file you want to protect visibly, or choose it.

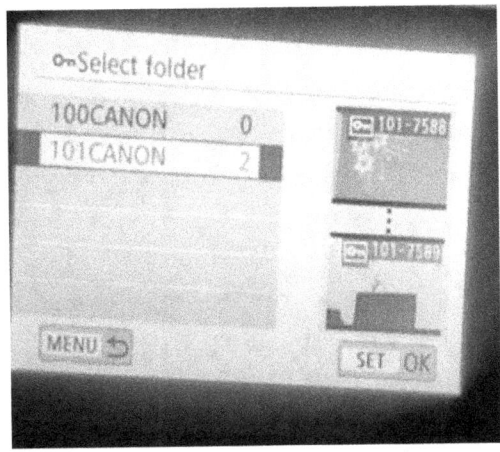

Then, only show the image (picture or video) in a single-image view.

- In 4/9/72 Thumbnail mode, move the yellow selection box over the file's thumbnail using the Multi Selector or Command dial. Next, select the file thumbnail in Calendar view from the thumbnail strip on the screen's right side. To switch between the calendar dates and the thumbnails.

Simply press the AE-L/AF-L button.

Check out the critical icon right by the button. You are now reminded to lock a photo using the button. During playback, photographs that are locked also display a key symbol.

Display or choose the file, then push the AE-L/AF-L button to remove the protection.

Chapter 5: Getting Creative with Exposure and Lighting

Introducing the Exposure Trio: Aperture, Shutter Speed, and ISO

Understanding exposure-setting side effects

A lens directs light onto a light-sensitive recording surface to produce a photograph. In a film camera, the film negative acts as that medium; in a digital camera, it's the image sensor, an advanced electrical component that analyzes light in a scene and transmits that data to the camera's data processing unit to produce an image. The aperture and shutter, two barriers between the lens and sensor of a digital camera, control how much light enters the sensor. As a result, the aperture, shutter, and sensor have different designs and arrangements in the digital world depends on the camera.

The image's exposure, or general brightness and contrast, is determined by the aperture, shutter, and a fourth element called ISO. The following is how the three-part exposure formula operates:

- **Aperture:** The aperture regulates the amount of light and is a movable hole in the lens's internal diaphragm. You can alter the aperture size to control the size of the light beam that can enter the camera.

Aperture settings are expressed as f-stop numbers, also known as just f-stops, written as f/2, f/5.6, f/16, and so on. The larger the aperture and the lower the f-stop number, the more light can enter the camera. (If using a higher number for a narrower aperture seems counterintuitive, consider this: A higher value generates a greater light barrier than a lower value.) Each lens has a different range of aperture settings.

- **Shutter speed (controls length of light):** The shutter operates similarly to window shutters. Until you push the shutter button, the camera's shutter remains closed, keeping light from reaching the image sensor (much as how closed window shutters keep sunlight out of a room). The shutter then briefly opens, allowing light from the aperture to reach the sensor. When you compose in Live View mode, this is an exception: When Live View is turned on, the shutter opens and stays open, allowing the image to develop on the sensor and be seen on the monitor. The shutter first closes when you push the shutter button; then, it opens again for exposure.

  In either case, the shutter speed—expressed in seconds—is the time the shutter is open to create the exposure: 1/250 second, 1/60 second, 2 seconds, and so on.

- **ISO (controls light sensitivity):** ISO allows you to change how sensitive the image sensor is to light. ISO is a digital feature rather than a mechanical component of the camera.

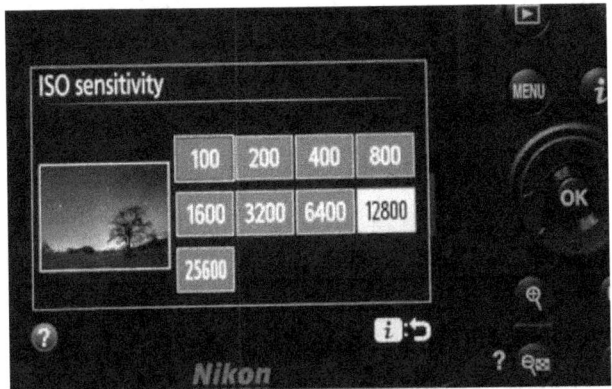

Doing the exposure balancing act.

Once more, adjusting these variables affects the picture in ways other than exposure:

- Depth of field is influenced by the aperture, with a larger f-stop number extending the range across which objects are sharp.

- Shutter speed determines whether the movement of the subject or the camera causes hazy images.

- ISO affects the camera's sensitivity to light. A faster shutter "freezes" action and also helps prevent all-over blur caused by camera shake when you handhold the camera. The camera responds to light better with a higher ISO, but there is a greater likelihood of image noise.

Recalling the soccer scenario, you must choose between the shallower depth of field that comes with a bigger aperture and the increased danger of noise that comes with a higher ISO if you want to increase the shutter speed to freeze the action.

Exploring the Advanced Exposure Modes

In the fully automatic exposure modes, you have little control over exposure. However, you can choose from one or two Flash modes. You can adjust ISO in the Scene modes and all Effects modes except Night Vision, But to gain full control over exposure, set the Mode dial to one of the advanced modes: P, S, A, or M. You also need to use these modes to take advantage of many other camera features, including some of its color and autofocus options.

Reading (And Adjusting) the Meter

The meter's minus sign represents underexposure and overexposure by the plus sign. You're good to go if there is only one vertical bar under 0 on the meter. However, you have an issue if there are any little bars to the left or right of the zero mark. The image will be overexposed if the bars appear to the right of 0. The image is underexposed if the bars are to the left of zero. Note the following details:

- The meter's marks denote exposure pauses. An exposure adjustment step is known as a stop. To double the light that can enter the camera with the present settings, you must increase exposure by one stop, which entails adjusting the aperture or shutter speed. You can utilize settings that allow only half as much light to reduce exposure by one stop. Increased or decreased ISO values also change the exposure by one stop.

On the viewfinder meter, the squares on either side of the 0 represent one full stop each. The little lines below, which only appear when the meter needs to alert over- or underexposure, divide each stop into thirds. The full-stop and third-stop positions on the meter are denoted by the taller and shorter bars, respectively. Once more, bars under the meter indicate the severity of the problem if the camera detects an exposure problem.

- If a triangle can be seen at the end of the meter, the over- or underexposure is more than the meter's two-stop range. In other words, you have a serious exposure problem.

- Remember that when exposure compensation is enabled, the meter indicates how much exposure adjustment is in effect. So, for instance, if you ask the camera to shoot a brighter image in your second photo, the meter will advise a one-stop overexposure. That's because by utilizing exposure compensation, you're overriding the camera's belief that its initial exposure settings were ideal.

Setting ISO, Aperture, and Shutter Speed

Adjusting the aperture and shutter speed

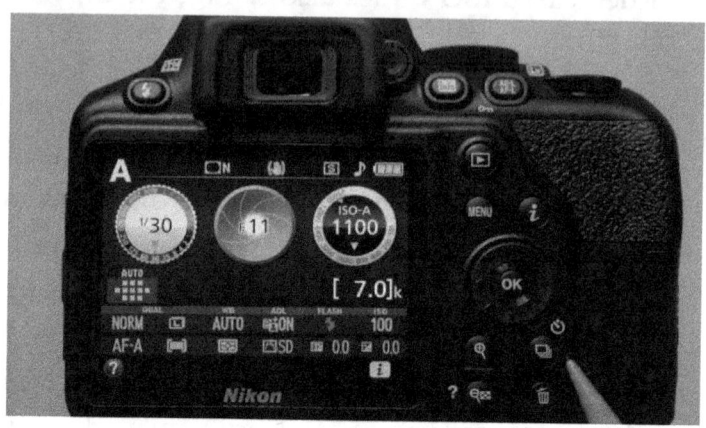

The current aperture (f-stop) and shutter speed can be seen in the viewfinder, the information display, and the live view display.

Start by pressing the shutter button halfway to activate the exposure system before choosing the aperture and shutter speed. The button can then be released. Depending on the exposure mode, the following step is as follows:

- **P (programmed auto exposure):** When you press the shutter button halfway, the camera shows you the appropriate f-stop and shutter speed. However, you can turn the Command dial to choose from various settings. The amount of combinations that can be made is determined by the camera's aperture settings, which are determined by your lens.

- **S (shutter-priority auto exposure):** Rotate the Command dial to select S (shutter-priority auto exposure) and adjust the shutter speed. As you move, the camera modifies the aperture as you move to preserve the desired exposure at the selected ISO.

  Except when the flash is used, shutter speeds range from 30 seconds to 1/4000 second. The maximum shutter speed when using flash is 1/200 second, whereas the lowest shutter speeds change based on the exposure setting. Due to how the camera must time the flash with the opening of the shutter, this restriction exists.

  When you change the shutter speed, the aperture value typically changes as well, making it simple to lose track of which setting you are in charge of. Just keep in mind that S mode controls the shutter speed. For A mode, the opposite is true, as is evident from the bullet point after that.

- **A (aperture-priority auto exposure):** Rotate the Command dial to change the f-stop setting using the preset of the A (aperture-priority auto exposure). The camera automatically chooses the right shutter speed to expose the photo at the selected aperture and ISO level.

  Your lens determines the range of f-stop settings that are possible. The range of zoom lenses often changes as you zoom in and out. For example, when set to its widest angle (shortest focal length), a lens might have a maximum aperture of f/3.5, yet it only allows you to zoom in to f/5.6. For information on the lowest and maximum aperture settings.

- **M (manual exposure):** Configure the shutter speed and aperture as follows:

    - Adjust the Command dial to change the shutter speed.

    - To change the aperture, turn the Command dial while pressing the Exposure Compensation button (located on top of the camera). Have you noticed the tiny symbol that resembles an aperture above the button? That serves as a reminder of how the button affects the f-stop while using M mode.

The settings the camera chooses in P, S, or A mode are determined by what it considers the right exposure. If you disagree, you can set the aperture and shutter speed to give you the desired exposure by switching the camera to manual exposure mode.

Controlling ISO

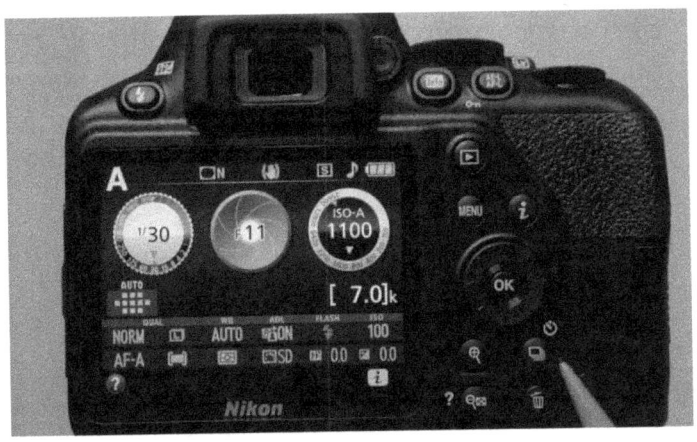

The ISO cannot be changed in the Auto and Auto Flash Off exposure modes; the camera automatically determines the ISO. Except for the Night Vision Effects mode, you can select ISO values between 100 and 25600 in any other exposure mode. You can also continue using Auto ISO and let the camera choose the acceptable ISO setting for the selected aperture and shutter speed.

Look in the Information and Live View screens to see the ISO setting. Only when the setting is set to Auto does the ISO information appear in the viewfinder. The words ISO AUTO will then appear on the viewfinder's right side, directly to the left of the Shots Remaining value. Otherwise, the viewfinder's ISO section is blank.

You may change ISO using one of these methods:

- **i button:** The control strip allows you to change the configuration.

- **Shooting menu:** The ISO Sensitivity Settings option on the Shooting menu also allows you to modify the setting. The top choice (ISO Sensitivity) is accessible in the other exposure modes. In either case, the choice determines the ISO level.

Choose ISO Sensitivity Settings from the Shooting menu, then click OK to make this option active. Next, set the Auto ISO Sensitivity Control option to On on the following screen.

Next, utilize these two menu choices to instruct the camera when to intervene and provide ISO support:

- **Maximum Sensitivity:** This feature allows you to choose how much noise potential you're willing to accept in exchange for good exposure. It sets the highest ISO the camera can use when it overrides the selected setting. This value is typically set to ISO 25600 (the maximum level on the D3500).

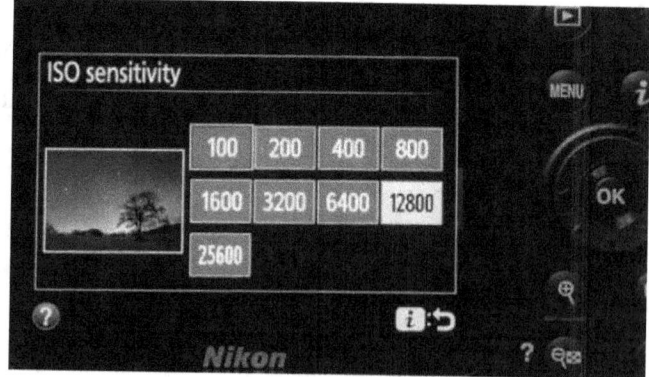

- **Minimum Shutter Speed:** Choose the minimum shutter speed at which the P and A exposure modes' ISO override kicks in. (In the M and S exposure modes, ISO is always modified as necessary to match the shutter speed and f-stop you have chosen.)

The ISO Auto label in the viewfinder and the Live View display blinks to warn you when the camera is ready to override your ISO setting. Additionally, the ISO image on the Information display blinks the message "ISO-A." Finally, if you utilize specific playback display modes, the ISO value displays in red when you examine your photos on the monitor. Set the Auto ISO Sensitivity Control option to Off to remove Auto ISO override.

Choosing an Exposure Metering Mode

You must be aware of the current Metering mode, which controls the area of the frame the camera examines to determine exposure to interpret what the exposure meter is telling you. The fully automatic shooting modes, P, S, and A modes of the camera, and the meter reading in M mode are all influenced by the metering mode.

Matrix: The camera examines the entire picture before choosing an exposure that will result in a balanced exposure.

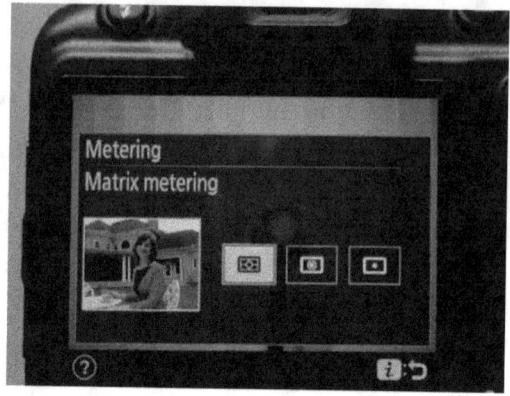

Center-weighted: The camera bases exposure on the entire frame but gives the center of the frame greater weight. In more detail, an 8mm circle in the middle of the frame receives 75% of the camera's metering weight.

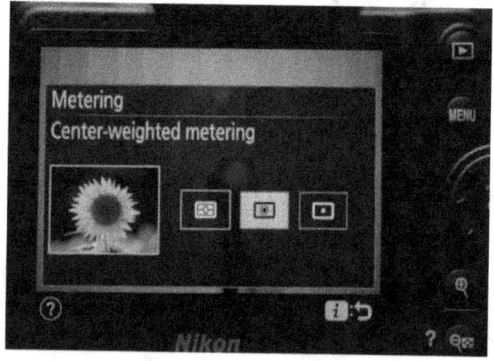

Spot: In this setting, the camera's exposure is completely based on a circular area that is approximately 3.5mm in diameter, or roughly 2.5 percent of the picture. The AF-area mode, an autofocusing option, determines the area used for this pinpoint metering. The autofocusing system will use which focal point on the camera is controlled by this setting. Here is how the setting impacts exposure:

- If you use other AF-area modes, which allow you to select a specific focus point, the camera bases exposure on that point.

- Exposure is based on the center focus point if you select the Auto Area mode, in which the camera selects the focus point for you.

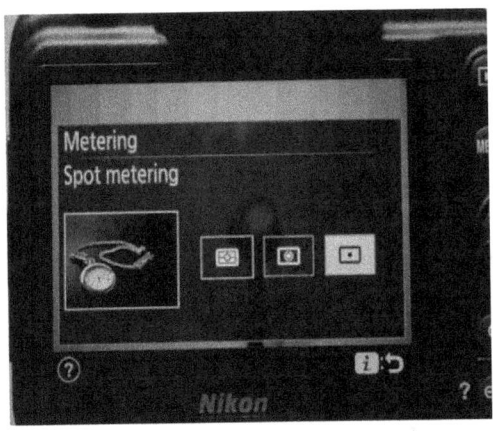

Applying Exposure Compensation

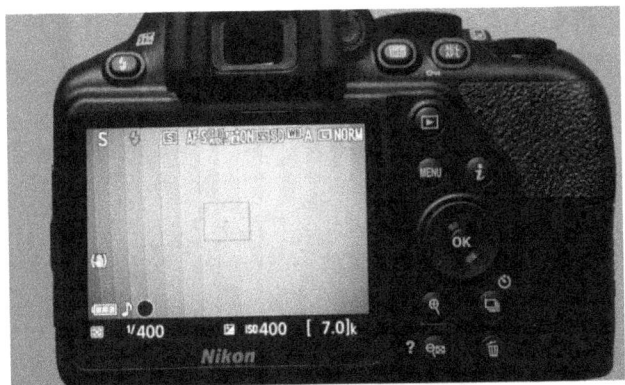

Not to worry: In the P, S, and A modes, you have the final say in an exposure. Exposure Compensation, a feature that instructs the camera to produce a brighter or darker exposure on your subsequent image regardless of whether you modify the aperture or shutter speed, is the trick (or both, in P mode).

When you enable exposure compensation, Nikon advises using either spot or center-weight metering for the best results. However, you don't have the patience to mess around with numerous settings when exposure is off. In that case, I advise focusing on exposure compensation and saving the metering mode option for another time.

Chapter 6: Putting It All Together

But remember that there aren't any absolute guidelines for taking a portrait, a landscape, or anything else. So allow yourself to explore on your own as you develop your creative vision by modifying this exposure setting or that focus control. After all, experimentation is a big part of what makes photography fun, and it's simple and cost-free due to your camera monitor and the Delete button.

Setting Up for Specific Scenes

Shooting still portraits

If your subject is in a still portrait, it must not be moving. Skip to the following section and employ the action photography techniques if your subject isn't interested in staying still. The traditional portraiture technique keeps the issue firmly focused while bringing the background into soft focus, assuming you have a subject ready to pose. This creative decision draws attention to the subject and lessens the prominence of distracting background elements.

You may obtain this appearance by following these instructions:

1. Choose a small f-stop value and set the Mode dial to A (aperture-priority autoexposure).

    The depth of field, or the distance over which focus appears to be acceptable sharp, is shortened when the aperture is opened by a low f-stop setting, letting more light into the camera. So the first step in softening your picture background is to dial in a low f-stop number.

2. Verify the focal length.

The best focal length for a traditional head-and-shoulders portrait is between 85 and 120mm. For portraits, avoid utilizing a short focal length (wide-angle lens). Similar to how people appear when viewed via a security peephole in a door, it can make features appear warped. Conversely, an excessively long focal length can flatten and expand a face.

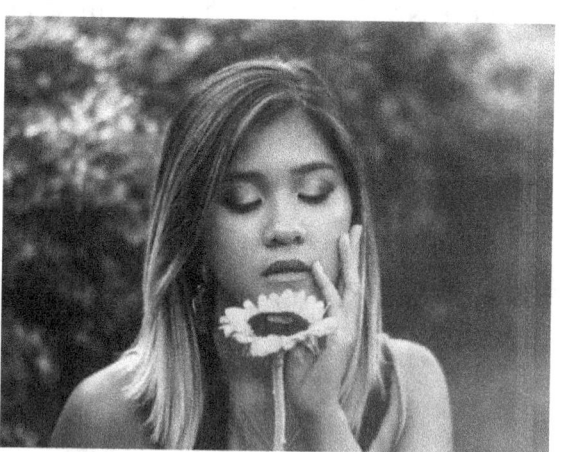

3. Increase the focus length, go closer to the subject, and increase the distance between the subject and the background to soften the background further.

The depth of field is decreased by zooming in or out or getting closer to your subject. Additionally, the background blurs more the farther away the subject is from it.

4. Verify the composition.

   Two simple tips on this subject:

   - Take history into account. Search the full frame for eye-catching backdrop elements. If possible and necessary, move the subject to a better-looking setting.

   - Crop the topic later to fit a range of frame sizes by framing it loosely. This is because the photographs that come out of your camera have a 3:2 aspect ratio. In other words, your photo must be cropped to print at other sizes, such as 5 x 7 or 8 x 10, even when it fits well as a 4- by 6-inch print.

5. If you can, avoid using flash when taking indoor portraits.

   Red-eye is avoided, and softer illumination is produced when shooting using available light rather than a flash. Posing your subject next to a sizable window during the day can result in images that resemble what you see.

6. Consider using flash when taking portraits outside during the day.

A flash can give subjects' faces a helpful pop of light. When the sun is directly overhead, casting severe shadows around the subject's eyes, nose, and chin, the background is brighter than the subject; the subject is wearing a hat or all above.

By pressing the Flash button in A exposure mode, you can activate the built-in flash (back of the camera, just left of the viewfinder). First, choose Fill Flash as the Flash option for daytime portraits. (That is the standard, fundamental Flash mode.) Next, try slow-sync flash or red-eye reduction for photographs taken at night; once more, go to the flash suggestions after these instructions for the best ways to employ each mode.

7. Hold the shutter button down while halfway pressing it to start exposure metering and autofocusing.

   You can manually focus by turning the lens's focusing ring.

8. Completely press the shutter button.

Capturing action

Any moving object, like a bicycle, a spinning Ferris wheel, or a flower in the breeze, can be captured in sharp focus using a quick shutter speed.

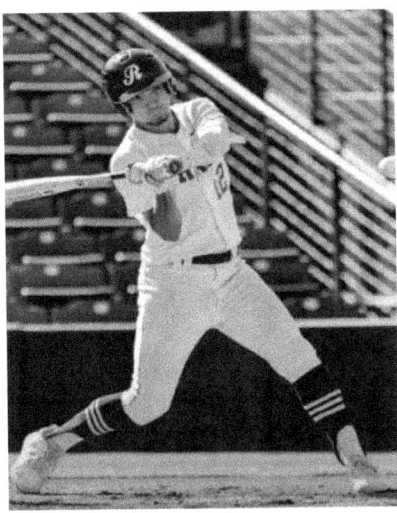

To capture a moving subject while still using the basic capture settings described before, use the methods in the subsequent steps:

1. Set S as the Mode dial (shutter-pri-ority auto exposure).

   In this mode, the camera chooses an aperture setting that will result in decent exposure while you control the shutter speed.

2. To adjust the shutter speed, turn the Command dial.

   Find the shutter speed in the viewfinder and information display.

   You must experiment to determine the proper shutter speed to capture motion because it depends on the subject's movement. However, save for the quickest subjects, 1/320 second ought to be plenty for most subjects (race cars, boats, and so on). You can even go as low as 1/250 or 1/125 second for sluggish-moving objects. Remember that the camera will expand the aperture to retain the same exposure when the shutter speed is increased. While the f-stop is low, the depth of field is shorter. Therefore, you must be extra attentive when framing and focusing the photo to maintaining your subject in the crisp focus area.

3. Think about increasing the ISO level to enable a faster shutter speed.

   Even if the camera opens the aperture as wide as possible, you might not be able to use a fast shutter speed at a low ISO unless you're shooting in broad daylight. Although increasing the ISO does increase the likelihood of noise, a little noise is typically preferable to a subject that is out of focus. In addition, when the ISO is increased, the camera may select an aperture that produces a deeper depth of field and makes it simpler to capture the subject in the area of the sharpest focus.

4. Change the Release mode to Continuous for rapid-fire shooting.

   As long as the shutter button is depressed, the camera records a continuous stream of shots in this mode. As a result, you may take as many as five pictures per second with the D3500. Again, though, you must avoid using the flash since, like with Single Frame release mode, you can only take one picture with each stroke of the shutter.

Pressing the Release Mode button on the camera's rear will give you quick access to the Release mode settings.

5. Choose options for quick focusing.

Autofocus can come in handy while working with a subject that moves, such as a bird in flight.

The two auto-focus settings are listed below:

- **Focus mode:** AF-C (continuous-servo autofocus).

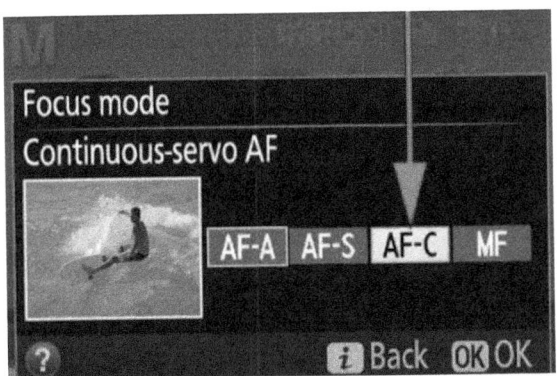

- **AF-area mode:** Dynamic Area.

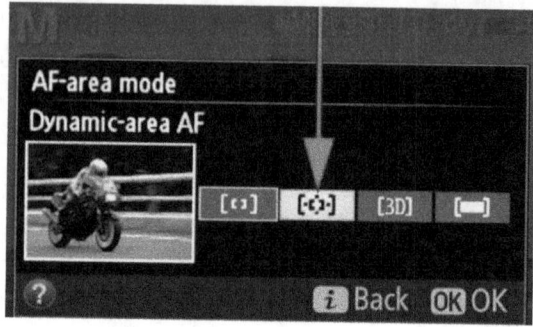

6. Position the subject so that it can move around the frame.

To reduce the likelihood that your subject may move out of the frame before you take the photo, frame your shot a little wider than you might ordinarily. Later, you can always crop to a more focused composition. It is also a good idea to leave more space in front of the subject than behind it. It makes it clear that your subject is moving in a specific direction.

Capturing scenic vistas

There is no one optimal method for photographing a stunning expanse of farmland, a city skyline, or any other large subject, making it difficult to provide precise capture settings for landscape photography. Most people prefer using a wide-angle lens to include a significant portion of the landscape in the image. Still, if you're close to your subject, you might like the results you get from a telephoto or medium-angle lens.

Another aspect of a great cityscape may be keeping every building in the frame vividly in focus. However, a different photographer might capture the same image so that one building in the foreground is sharply emphasized while the others are less, calling attention to that initial structure.

Here are some pointers to assist you in capturing a scene as you see it:

- Use the aperture-priority autoexposure mode (A) to regulate the depth of field when taking pictures. Choose a high f-stop number if you want an extremely shallow depth of field so that both nearby and faraway objects are sharply focused. Use a low f-stop number for shallow depth of field. Remember that depth of field is also influenced by the lens's focal length and the distance between the camera and the subject: The background grows hazier when you zoom in or use a longer focal length.

- Think about using a slow shutter speed to get that "misty" effect in photographs of dramatic waterfalls. As a result of the slow shutter, the water appears soft and romantically blurred. The photo's shutter speed was 1/5 of a second.

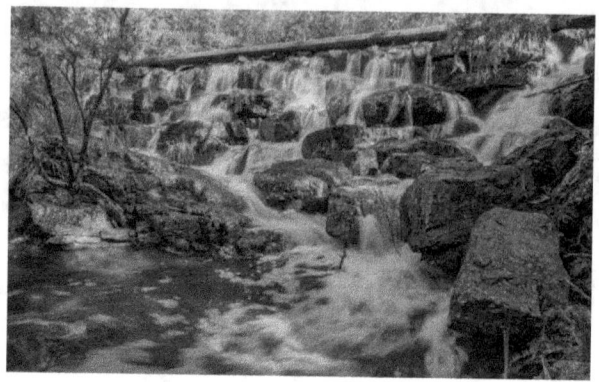

- Use a tripod if the exposure calls for a slow shutter speed. Any camera movement during the exposure blurs the entire frame; thus, if you try to handhold the camera, you can end up with a lousy photo. Instead, try turning on the Optical VR feature, which is located in the Shooting menu, if you don't have a tripod and cannot find other ways to stabilize the camera. When using specific lenses, such as the AF-P kit lens, this option helps to account for slight camera movement (the VR stands for vibration reduction). Some lenses have an external switch for turning on and off a corresponding feature, including Nikon's AF-S lenses. (The switch is designated as VR on Nikon lenses.)

- When shooting at sunrise or sunset, consider the sky. The foreground will be dark, but if necessary, you can make it brighter in a photo editor. On the other hand, the sky will become so bright that all the color will be washed out if you base exposure on the foreground, a problem you typically can't fix after the fact. Another option is a graduated neutral density filter, which changes from dark to clear. The filter is placed so that the clear portion covers the area with low light and the dark portion covers the sky. With this setup, you can better expose the foreground without overexposing the hues of the sky.

Try out Active D-Lighting as well; it can be used to produce images with a wider range of brightness values than is typically feasible.

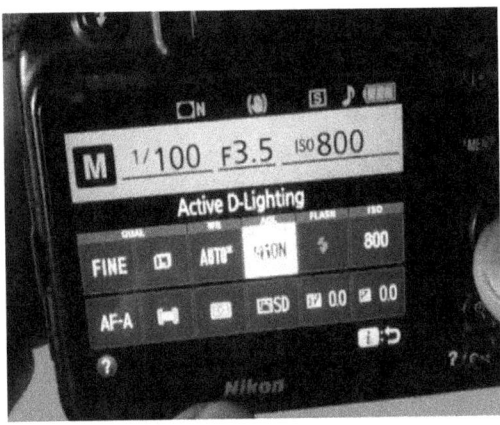

- Experiment with slow shutter speeds for interesting nighttime city photos. Assuming that cars or other vehicles with their lights are moving through the landscape, the effect is neon light trails like those you see in the photograph's foreground. The shutter speed for this shot was roughly 10 seconds.

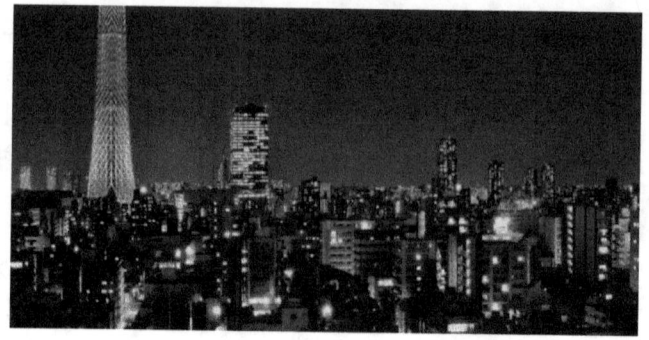

- For the finest illumination, they were photographed during the magic hours. Photographers refer to those times of day—early morning and late afternoon—when the sun's light gives everything a lovely, gently warmed appearance.

- Brace your exposures under tricky lighting.

By taking the same photo at various exposure settings or bracketing, you can enhance the likelihood that at least one of them will capture the scene you had in mind. When the illumination is poor, like at sunrise and sunset, bracketing is a good idea, more than usual.

The best way to bracket exposures when using the M exposure mode is to adjust the shutter speed rather than the f-stop between each image. It will ensure that the depth of field, which is partly influenced by the f-stop, is constant across all of your photographs.

You can use various Exposure Compensation settings for each shot while utilizing the P, S, and A exposure modes to bracket exposures. For example, consider three images: one with no exposure compensation, one with exposure compensation set to +1.0, and one with exposure compensation set to -1.0. Press and hold the Exposure Compensation button on top of the camera while turning the Command dial to set the exposure compensation value.

- Include a foreground topic in wide-angle landscape shots to give the viewer a feeling of scale.

Capturing dynamic close-ups

Try these methods for fantastic close-up pictures:

- To determine the minimum close focusing distance, consult the manual. Your lens, not the camera body, dictates how "up close and personal" you can get with your subject.

- Change the camera's mode to A (aperture-priority auto exposure mode) to regulate the depth of field. The focal point of your photograph will determine whether you like a shallow, medium, or extreme depth of field.

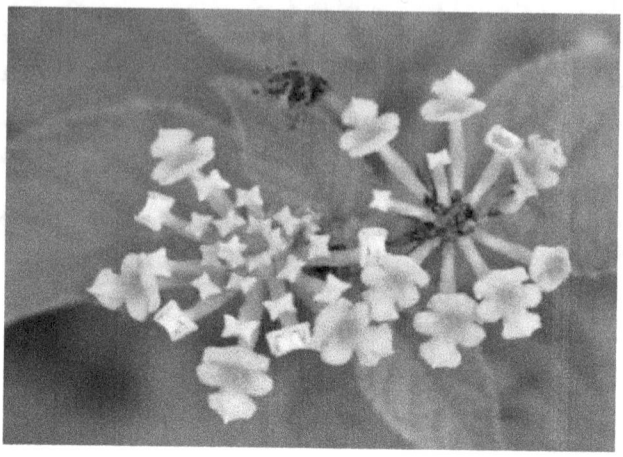

- Keep in mind that as you zoom in or go closer to your subject, the depth of field gets less. Return to the product shot: You may need to go farther away, zoom out, or do both if you require more depth of focus than what the aperture setting can provide. (You may always crop your photo only to include the components of the subject you wish to highlight.)

- Shutter speed should also be considered when photographing flowers and other natural landscapes outside. For example, your subject could move with a moderate breeze, which will blur the image at slow shutter rates.

- Try using a flash to improve outside lighting. Similar to portraits, close-ups occasionally benefit from a small amount of flash when the sun is the primary light source. The maximum shutter speed that may be used when using the built-in flash is 1/200 second, so bear that in mind once more. If the light is particularly bright, you should use a high f-stop setting to prevent the photo from being overexposed at the maximum shutter speed. Through the Flash Compensation control, the flash output can also be modified.

- Avoid using the built-in flash as your main light source when you're pretty close to the subject when shooting indoors. Even if you use the Flash Compensation function to lower flash strength, the light from your flash may still be too harsh when used up close. Instead, if flash is unavoidable, turn on as many room lights as possible to lower the required flash power. (You might need to adjust the White Balance setting if you have a variety of light sources, though.)

- Buy a macro lens or a pair of diopters if you want to get up close and personal with your topic. For example, if you're not into nature photography, you can catch details of an object using a macro lens, which allows you to concentrate at a very close range.

A good macro lens can cost from a few hundred to several thousand dollars. But it's worth the cost if you like to document the little things in life.

For a less expensive option, you can spend approximately $40 on a set of diopters, like reading glasses that you clamp onto your lens. Diopters are available in various strengths, with higher numbers signifying stronger magnification (+1, +2, +4, etc.). In addition, you may add a diopter on top of another in most setups to boost power.

The drawback of a diopter is that it frequently results in photographs with highly soft edges; this is fine with a decent macro lens.

Chapter 7: Downloading, Organizing, and Archiving Your Picture Files

Sending Pictures to the Computer

Connecting the camera and computer

If you decide to purchase the USB cable required to link your camera and computer for direct photo download, follow these instructions to do so:

1. Verify the camera's battery life. Charge the battery if necessary before moving on. Loss of image data can occur if the battery runs out during the downloading process. If the AC adapter was purchased, use it to power the camera while it is being downloaded.

2. Switch on the computer and give it time to complete the typical startup process.

3. Disconnect the camera.

4. Place the smaller two connectors on the USB cord into the camera's USB port.

   For this port, look underneath the door on the left-hand side of the camera.

5. Connect the cable's opposite end to a USB port on the computer.

6. Start the camera.

What happens next depends on the photo software you have installed on your computer. The options and how to carry out the transfer process are described in the next section.

7. After the download is finished, switch off the camera and unplug it from the computer.

Starting the transfer process

What happens next once you connect the camera to the computer or place a memory card in a card reader depends on the software set up on your computer. However, the most typical scenarios and next steps are as follows:

- You notice a message on a Windows PC asking what application you wish to use to download your images (or movies). If you don't already have a preferred program for this job, go with Nikon ViewNX-i. Once you've installed the program on your computer, it ought to be accessible as an option. The following are instructions for downloading files using this program.

- An installed photo software immediately shows a photo download wizard. For instance, on a Mac, you might see the downloader connected to Photos (or iPhoto, on systems running some older versions of the Mac OS). Another photo-related downloader, like the one for Adobe Lightroom, might come to the fore. The downloader that appears is typically connected to the program that you just installed.

- Nothing occurs. Relax; everything should be OK, given that your card reader or camera is connected properly. It's possible that someone on your machine simply disabled all of the automated downloaders. Start your photo-editing program, and then use the command to transfer your images.

Downloading and Organizing Photos with the Nikon Software

Downloading with Nikon Transfer

Nikon Transfer, a built-in tool for downloading files, is part of Nikon ViewNX-i. To preview and download pictures and movies from your memory card, follow these steps:

1. If Nikon Transfer 2 still needs to be opened, start it now.

    The Nikon Transfer 2 window can pop up immediately when you connect the camera to the computer or insert your memory card into a card reader, depending on how ViewNX-i was set up. Start ViewNX-i, and select Import Images with Transfer from the File menu if you can't see the Nikon Transfer 2 popup. You can select Import from the menu at the top of the ViewNX-i window.

2. Open the Source tab to see thumbnails of your photos.

    Are no tabs visible? To see them, click the Options triangle. Click the Source tab next. Next, you should choose the icon for your camera or memory card. Click the icon and select the device that contains the files you wish to transfer if your camera or card isn't already chosen.

3. Make your choice among the files you want to download.

To choose a file for download, click a thumbnail to highlight it. Then, click the box in the file's lower-right corner. These methods quicken the procedure:

- Only choose protected files. By selecting the Select Protected icon, you can only choose the photos you protected with the in-camera feature.

- Choose every file. Select All by clicking the similarly labeled icon in the illustration.

4. To see options for processing the file transfer, click the Primary Destination tab.

The Primary Destination Folder controls where the software stores your transferred files; it is the most crucial setting on this tab. (Seek out the option on the tab's left side.) Next, choose the folder on your computer's hard disk (or external drive) from the drop-down list by opening it.

You can also choose whether to rename files during the transfer and how photographs should be arranged inside the main destination folder using the other options on this tab.

5. Click the Backup Destination tab to see your options for sending copies of your photos to a backup disk in addition to your primary storage location. This feature saves time-saving by allowing you to simultaneously download images to your main disk and a backup drive. Use the other panel options to determine where you want the backup files to go after checking the Backup Files box,

6. To see the available options, click the Preferences tab.

    Here, three settings are crucial:

    - Transfer New Files Only: Selecting this option prevents you from wasting time downloading pictures that have already been transmitted.

      Turn off the "Delete Original Files after Transfer" option. Otherwise, your photos are deleted from your memory card after the transfer is finished. Before deleting photos from your memory card, always be sure they were transferred to the computer.

    - After Transfer, Open Destination Folder with the Following Application: You can instruct the program to launch your photo editing software immediately. Use the application ViewNX-i to browse and catalog your photos.

To select a different application, open the drop-down list, select Browse from the dialog box that displays, and then select the desired program. After that, click OK.

You only need to return to this tab once you wish the application to act differently because whatever options you select here are effective for all subsequent download sessions.

7. Click the Start Transfer button in the Nikon Transfer 2 window at the bottom.

The Process bar in the lower-left corner of the program window displays the transfer status once you press the button. The choices you made in Step 6 will determine what happens after the transfer is finished. For example, if you choose Nikon ViewNX-i as the photo program, it will open and show the folder containing the images you just downloaded.

Viewing picture metadata

You can select from several display modes in a single-image picture view, and each one shows different shooting information alongside the image or first frame of a movie file. Press the Multi Selector up and down to switch from one display to the next while the recording is being played.

The Playback Display Options item on the Playback menu must be enabled to use the other modes; the File Information mode is the only one accessible by default.

A feature is activated when a checkmark appears in the box next to it. By selecting the choice and then pressing the Multi Selector to the right, you may turn the checkmark on and off. Press OK after activating the settings you want to use.

Processing RAW (NEF) Files

Processing RAW images in the camera

You can convert a Raw file directly in the camera to a JPEG format by selecting the NEF (RAW) Processing option from the Retouch menu. Take these actions:

1. To enter playback mode, press the Playback button.

2. Show the image in full-frame mode.

    By selecting OK, you can change the view from thumbnails to a single image if necessary. If you're in the Calendar view, press OK twice.

3. Depress the I key.

    The i-button menu is displayed on the screen.

4. To reveal the Retouch menu, highlight Retouch and press the Multi Selector to the right.

5. Scroll to the option for NEF (RAW) Processing.

6. To see your processing options, press OK.

   You get a screen where you can tell the camera what parameters to use when producing the JPEG version of the Raw image. The second page of options scrolls when you depress the Multi Selector.

7. Choose your conversion settings.

   You may find the conversion options in a column on the right side of the screen. Pressing the Multi Selector to the right after selecting an option will show the available settings. Select what you want, then click OK to go back to the main Raw conversion screen. You can use the Multi Selector's right button to see more possibilities if a triangle appears to the right of a setting name.

   The list that follows provides some general advice if you are unfamiliar with all the settings:

   - **Image Quality:** Select Fine to maintain the best possible picture quality.

   - **Image Size:** Select Large to keep every pixel from the source image.

   - **White Balance:** Use the Auto setting unless the colors seem off. Otherwise, try out each setting to determine which appropriately produces colors.

- **Exposure Compensation:** You can change the image's brightness with this option. When using this feature for Raw conversion, your options are limited to a range between -2.0 and +2.0; however, when shooting, your options are between nd5.0 and +5.0. For a brighter image, increase the value; for a darker image, decrease it.

- **Picture Control:** This option can change color saturation, contrast, and sharpness. The screen changes to show you the results of the chosen Picture Control, much like the White Balance and Exposure Compensation settings.

- **High ISO Noise Reduction:** If your image appears noisy or speckled, turning on this feature may help.

- **Color Space:** This choice controls whether the camera converts your image using the smaller Adobe RGB color space or the bigger sRGB color space.

- **Vignette Control:** Are the corners of your image unnaturally dark? Applying the Vignette Control feature might occasionally erase or at least lessen this issue, known as vignetting.

- **D-Lighting:** Try modifying this setting to lighten the darkest portion of your image without simultaneously brightening the lightest areas. The equivalent of the active D-lighting function may be used when shooting in post-production. For example, try setting the option to Off if you want to lighten shadows. In addition, you can adjust the level of adjustment to High, Normal, or Low.

By using the Zoom In button, you can enlarge the image whenever you like using the Zoom In button. Press and hold the button until the display returns to normal.

8. Click OK after selecting EXE on the first conversion screen.

Your Raw file is copied into a JPEG by the camera, which displays the copy on the monitor. The original file number and the processed JPEG file number do not match because the camera allocates the next available file number to the image. During playback, you can also see the tiny Retouch menu icon (the box with a paintbrush).

Processing RAW files in ViewNX

Although I altered the window layout to show before and after views of my shot and to present the panel of Raw conversion options down the right side of the window.

You can change these, and other application window features through choices on the View and Window menus. To access the tools available for modifying your Raw image, click the Edit tool tabs.

No matter what you do, you can't really "damage" your picture, so don't be scared to experiment. Also, since you can only make a copy of your original data in the TIFF or JPEG formats, your original data is never overwritten.

The following advice should get you off to a good start:

- First, click on the Raw file. Next, click the thumbnail of the image you want to edit after starting Capture NX-D. Next, open the View menu, then choose the Thumbnail option if you don't see any thumbnails.

- Show your photo's before-and-after perspectives. Once more, the View menu holds the key to changing the screen layout. First, select Compare Before and After photos to place your original and altered versions of the image side by side. Next, select Preview from the View menu to conceal thumbnails for additional photographs. Finally, launching the Window menu and selecting the Folders and Bird's Eye options can further clear the clutter screen. (Clicking the options causes the corresponding panels to be shown or hidden.)

- Make the editing tools visible. Along the right side of the window are controls for modifying your Raw image. Open the Window menu and select Edit. From the menu, select Retouch to bring up a second panel of tools.

- To view the many editing tools categories, click the labeled adjustment icons. If more options are required, scroll the display using the scroll bar on the right side of the window.

- Choose the tools at the program's top to crop and straighten the image. First, drag a line that has to be vertical or horizontal with the Straighten tool. When you select the Crop tool, a crop box will appear. To crop, drag the crop box's edges. (When you pick a different tool, the crop is applied.)

- From the top drop-down selection on the Edit panel, select Recorded Settings to reverse all of your changes. After you make your initial adjustment to the image, the term Manual should appear in the list. Selecting Recorded Settings returns you to the beginning and shows the image as it was initially.

- Open the File menu and select Convert Files after altering the image. The processed version of your original Raw image is created in this phase. Next, set the Save as Type and File Format options to TIFF and 8-bit TIFF in the resulting Save dialog box. (You might be unable to utilize the image in other apps, like Microsoft PowerPoint, if you select 16-bit TIFF.) The different choices operate similarly to when you save files in most Mac or Windows programs: Give the file a name, specify the location where you want to put it, and then click Save.

www.ingramcontent.com/pod-product-compliance
Lightning Source LLC
Chambersburg PA
CBHW070256220526
45465CB00004B/1634